WOLF
LAMB
BOMB

WOLF
LAMB
BOMB

poems
Aviya Kushner

Print ISBN: 978-1-949039-17-7
Ebook ISBN: 978-1-949039-18-4

Orison Books
PO Box 8385
Asheville, NC 28814
www.orisonbooks.com

Distributed to the trade by Itasca Books
1-800-901-3480 / orders@itascabooks.com

Cover art: "Meir Shfeyah, 2016." Acrylic on canvas (40" x 30").
Copyright © 2016 by Assaf Shani. Used with permission of the artist.
www.assafshaniart.wixsite.com/assafshaniart

Manufactured in the U.S.A.

ORISON
BOOKS

CONTENTS

A voice rings out: "Proclaim!"

Another asks, "What shall I proclaim?"

All flesh is grass,

All its goodness like flowers of the field:

–Isaiah 40:6
*translated from the
Hebrew by H. L Ginsberg*

The Book of Isaiah

For years I wanted to be that angry,
and for it to be that beautiful.
I loved the poetry of rage.

And now, all I can remember are the hills:
I can hear the fire in them, words shaking earth. Even a bull
knows its owner, an ass its master.
Hear, heavens. Give ear, oh Earth.

I.

A Voice Rings Out

Music

Like a lyre my head moans
for the girls who are taken, the young
wives—and I cannot decide
if I too want to be a wife,
bound and also protected,
or if I would rather be a lone
crooner in the wilderness,
there not by choice but by
a wire, a flame,
a pillar, a force of earth.
Art is a religion, some say,
with a sad nod of their heads,
but I think it is also a wife
and husband, a God and servant,
friend and sweet master, music and moan.

Rumor

There's a crazy man in those hills,
howling that he can comfort us all.
There's an old crazy man in all of us,
saying I raised you, made you tall,
and you—you, rebellious little wuss,
you forgot that an ox knows who owns
him, an ass knows his place. Rain falls
and we rain blame, the way our ancestors
rained blame. Bombs explode in a faraway
city where I once lived, and the world rains
its curses on man, on God, on the whole idea
of *I will be what I will be, I am what I am,*
forget tenses because I am past and present
and future, and I breathed you
into you. Listen, someone once said—
I am comforting you, breathing
through an old, towering prophet
who is nothing but a singer on a stage,
a singer when there is only one
light left, and the soft illusion of a face.
In a few years you too will be just rumor,
a fire, dry grass, a singer who sang and then
disappeared from the lilt of performance,
the light of the audience, the light of the world.
A balm to the crazy, the rebel, the wuss—
Isaiah to the nations of the earth.
Like the tale of an old crazy man in the hills,
a song and a howl, a wolf and a lamb,
a story everyone claims.

Stubble

Was Isaiah,
my favorite of the poets,
bearded at the end?

Did he ever rebel against himself
with a razor, a foreign
language, a move
to a faraway continent—

like his descendants?
Or did he
just prophesy?

In the imagined life,
the next step is always
a problem.

Isaiah Starts It Up

This is the harshest of the ten tongues men call prophecy,
this is the dream of Isaiah the son of Amotz,
this is the seen, the eye, the vision,
this is the point where you're not sure if it's sanity or hallucination
or finally, actual and alarming truth,
and no I won't tell you what tribe I'm from or what land
I represent, because I'm all tribes, all lands, all women, all men,
so shimu shamayim v'haazini aretz, ooh-ooh-ooh,
listen heavens and eavesdrop, earth,
sit there and cower and hide in the corner,
use the desert as cover and the rain as disguise,
listen to me oh listening heavens
and envelop me, eavesdropping earth,
corn, wheat, soybeans, and sod,
listen until you forget yourself, so you can bless, confess, bless
the bare plains and the blank fields
and become all eye in the belly of man.

Smoke

God will empty the land of you—
the sword will rule your fields,
Sennacherib will come and remove
ten-twelfths of you, and you'll cry,

oh you will cry, and you'll say, this is the end,
there is no more, but no,
this is the beginning of comfort.

And I remember the days after the disaster:
how quiet it was on the highways,
how drivers let others pass,
how even the Hudson seemed to mourn,
and how we began to be thankful,

for mother and father and land and wallet,
in that order,
and how the smoke was followed
by a mild winter,
and how everything seemed more
beautiful, I suppose,
and temporary, after the sword, after the worst.

The Earth Is Tottering

The drivers on the highway
look dazed, and I want to yell—

go back to the beginning,
when this earth was wild and waste,
when you were a nude thought, an inkling,
when the wind was fluttering over the water—

remove everything you thought you had,
waste yourselves to the bone and stare:

I have stared.
For months after a bomb
vomited orange flame
out of a little white car
in front of my apartment in Jerusalem,
shaking that car
into a smoldering black husk,

and in the months after the tall buildings
in the first city I knew became dust—
I asked: *Am I the woman I want to be?*
Haunting were the answers.

At night, yes.
At night I have always been at home.
My voice gets deeper, I feel the earth beneath
my feet, I feel the movement of the darkness.
But in the day, I am more waste than wild.

I was tottering for years and only see
it now, my hair thinned, my body bare,
my faith in the sun stripped to nothing,

my whole world slow as the totter
of continents: ancient, eternal drift.

Nails

Right after a bombing, I'd walk and walk and walk, and stare
at the ancient stones, some covered in moss, all coated
in a light somewhere between holiness and rose-white, and a spare

song would come to me, every time—
as I waited to hear if someone who was mine
was now gone, now slime

and smoke and ash. Sometimes the song was comprehensible,
sometimes not, sometimes the rat-poisoned nails scattered
by the bomb made it impossible

to think, but not tonight, not this night of nights.
How is this night different
from other nights?

That's what I was taught to ask as a girl,
that's how I was taught to remember Exodus,
the great parting of the sea between slavery

and freedom, beast of burden and breathing human.
If I answered now, if someone stopped and bothered
to ask me *How is this night different from other nights?*

I'd say, or I'd sing, maybe I'd tap it against
the stones—tonight we are all aged, worn from the wrinkles of nails
lining this street; tonight we are too afraid

to sing, to clap, to become happily toothless
and slowly old. Tonight a fat religious man
in the overpriced bookstore on the corner

of King George Street handed me

the Book of Isaiah, and said,
This is a nice edition. And it was.

He was flush with flesh
and belief in words.
I thanked him, ran home to hear the latest

of the ancient—
thinking, why not read something so old
it doesn't matter?—
and in the background, the fires
engulfing all of us, here, now, still alive.

I waited for the call.
I waited to be told the dead-
line. This was one of those nights
when I was paid to interview Jerusalemites,
to ask my neighbors
questions with no answer.

How did you feel when you heard?—
        Was there something different
some feeling you had
        that tonight was different from other nights?

And as I waited I thought of the old
story of Exodus, the old idea of a promise
between God
and man, God and woman,

and I thought of all the singers
on all the stages of the earth
singing about promises unkept,
promises shattered—

II.

Proclaim!

Stupor

I'm gonna thank you one day because you got angry
at me. I'm gonna crawl back now, and I wouldn't
have had to crawl on all fours if you hadn't hit me.

Which is how my grandfather lived; after his four
brothers were killed, and his parents, too, he gardened
on Yom Kippur. But when his wife was struck too—

thirty-six and lovely she was, at her death. So he came back
to God. Like Job my grandfather was, the only one to live
to tell, a man who talked directly to the heavens, who asked

why and then didn't explode from the question. And I know
something within me, something that saw that first headless man
and the ones who followed, something that saw the burning

bodies of Jerusalem erupt, and the first city I knew crumble;
something that saw the white sign flying over the entrance to the ancient
city proclaiming *Jerusalem, do not fear*, something that was in my grandfather

lives; "I have lived to tell thee," which means I alone is sad
but not really right: one day I will finally stop gardening, will tumble
out of my stupor and say, I am angry, I am raving mad,

14

you have taken so much from me, and yet I know you last
as my song, my friend, the maker of the sea, creator of the sun,
the human, the hard wind and the garden and the land.

The Wind

How can I explain the wind to you?
It flutters, it flirts
with the water in the opening
lines of Genesis.

And then it comes back,
the way everything important
comes back, but as the wind of wisdom,
the wind of God, the wind of understanding—

"Spirit," you say. "You're explaining
the spirit of God."

Not exactly.
I want to hold your hand, and explain it to you
softly, "ruach"—

listen to how the wind has ooh
and aah in it. More than air,
that wind on water, fluttering—
not just God
but something of God:
like man, like woman,
like the world.

Storm Suite

In the wildest rain, Isaiah comes back.
Speak to Jerusalem, speak to her heart,
oh speak even from Iowa, from the soft
gray hills and the black plains of winter,
from the sudden valley of the frozen Mississippi,
from wherever you are,
and from whatever ends of earth you have claimed
for yourself—
speak from where you have been planted,
and tell her that her suffering is over,
her day is done.

In this rain,
in this whipping wilderness
of February,
you sway, a weed in the wind of God,
your throat tightening,
your belly growling in hunger, in submission,
and an old man flirts
bravely, anyway, his face open and cryptic,
teeth yellow and determined
like an aging prophet,
right hand shaking, and the rain falls
like a curse on him
as he talks, a watery, wobbly malediction,
but still he tries to swim
into the world
of a young woman, his lips swishing
the words *you are so sensual, you are so sensuous,*
and the rain
makes everything float,
compliments and cars suddenly
frictionless in the angry waters.

Comfort o comfort,
Isaiah tries, somewhere in the back of your mind,
and *I have been watching you,*
the old man whispers, rasping against the water,
but nothing is comforted
and nothing is owned.
And still he smiles, all yellow teeth.
I cannot give you
what you want, you say, softly,
soft as water,
but the man is already weeping,
tears in his shaking hand.

What he wants
is wild darkness,
the wild we all think we want until
we have it: the wild of memory,
the wild that lets Isaiah come back, raging,
screaming again in the mind and in the water,
in the emptiness of Iowa,
his rants reaching where we have been
and wherever we are going.

I cannot give, you say again,
and suddenly another man,
a man from Jerusalem, a small man
exhausted by war, grayed by escape,
comes to say that his car died last night
in this water, here in the exile of Iowa;
the old man stares as the small man tells
how he watched his escape sink in this puddle
of mud, wash of divine wrath. You know
you have seen what he has seen:
flying arms, a head tottering after
the explosion in the market,
an old woman wailing, insane at the end,
wild in her anger at God, at the holy city.
You think of explaining this
to the old man in simple, declarative English,
but your mouth is dry and your hands are wet.

Take me out
of this wild, Isaiah. The more it rains
the more I understand the old man,
and the less I can speak to him.
The more it rains the more I want
a love of my own, a love I have
chosen,
which is what he wants,
and the more it rains
the more I want
the certainty
and flood
of prophecy, the words to tell
what the watery future will
contain—

The old man
looks at me and knows
these things are chosen for you, not chosen
by you; he winks because
something in whatever our future is
weighs more than flirtation
and less than prophecy,
and whatever will be will be light,
soft and soothing as water from God,
and angry as rain, too.
He winks
because he knows what all rain is,
anger we know we deserve, deep down,
anger like the anger of Isaiah saying—
I am not talking to you, but to your heart,
to the insides of your city, to the capital
of yourself.

The old man's eyes are wet,
and in the wild rainstorm
tonight come the tears
of the angel who held back the hand
of Abraham, the father of all our fathers,
as he prepared to sacrifice his only son—
those tears are here, tonight, right now,
and you, the daughter of the stars,
daughter of Abraham's descendants,
daughter of all the grains of sand
across the width of earth,
you hear the words leave your home,
leave, just leave, and you do, over and over again,
you wait for that place
that God will show you again,
and again.

And in the wild of tonight
in the wildness of this blackness
is the stubbornness of the rock
that Moses turned to water,
and in the rain
is the split water of the Red Sea,
what was before heaven and earth
split into two beings,
flat and curved,
plains and valley, dwelling
and possibility, because once
we all lived in the possible,
back in the beginning of the beginning,
that even Isaiah never got to see—
when everything was water.

III.

Another Asks:
What Shall I Proclaim?

Talking Back to Isaiah

Oh man, let me be—
I want to weep, I want to take
my high-heeled sandals off and walk
in the desert, my personal and terrible country
of lust and poverty and want,
my hot and punishing span of dust and blankness,
dangers and ambush and wind.

I have heard the throaty prophecy.
Your words have snaked across centuries,
crossed canyons and chasms,
have gone from man to girl to woman;
your roar has reached its destination.
Lie back now, lie back.

Let your words float into the new
mouth of the future, its air.
You say your night of pleasure
has been God-flipped to terror
and I say, what was the night?

"Blackness," you say. I want to know
if there even was a thing called night
before God gave it to you.
Was the night of pleasure you sing
about the one of darkness and explosion,
of bodies incinerated to bits, to heads
and rolling parts, the most public
of humiliations, the quivering dead tongue?

Was it the night of the seven years of waiting
or the seven years of knowledge?

I know all about the seven years of fatness,
of good fields, and then the dryness of wheat,
the thinness of the sad stalks.
It was all dreamed of before my time.

Dear guide, dear eternal rival—
do not try, always, to walk into my dreams.
Do not tell me you have seen this all before,
that Assyria never dies, just returns in disguise,
in hot breath instead of cold breath,
in a new language of old violence.

Oh let me be. I am not the watchman,
to be beckoned at all hours to do your will.
I cannot compete with your wild flips,
your pyrotechnics of wolves, lambs, seraphim,
wings beating into the face, and the back, and the air.

I can only carry your words inside me,
like swallowed diamonds smuggled
into the crevices of the body for safekeeping,
I can only work to hear what you say you heard
and squint to see what you say you saw.

I am taking my sandals off now,
I am baring my feet to the desert,
I am letting the hot sand burn the bottoms
of what I will walk on for the rest of my life.

Here, I have tried to walk with you,
to walk sandaled and proper.
I imagine the ancient sometimes,
I can walk with the sway of a woman
of three thousand years ago,
with her jeweled bangles and the heft
of her long skirts, her hips, her hair,
I can descend into the valleys of your ancient hills.
I can stand in the outskirts of Jerusalem

and tell myself I will be an outsider
for the rest of my life, gazing toward the golden city.

Now let me dress myself in the green leaves
of the future. Go back
to the books now,
and let me be.

Isaiah Gets Feisty

And on that day the ram's horn
will be blown, u'vau ha'ovdim—and the lost will come
from Assyria, oh yeah, and the forgotten from
Egypt, vehaneedachim m'eretz mitzraim.
and then you little woman of earth will remember God,
then his headdress will look glorious to you, suddenly,
and then you will say to find what I want
I must return, must come back,
must free myself through my past.
Go learn from Sennacherib, fat king who thought he conquered
with his muscles, go look at the foolish Egyptians,
who thought pyramids meant permanent strength.
You sit and think words will protect you. Oh who
can collect you from the corners of the earth?
Adonai izuz v'gibor, God is brave and muscular,
God is the brave of war, the keeper of the tongues.
Open the gates to your head, your heart,
return from your personal Assyria, your endless Egypt.

Why Don't You Write in Hebrew?

Because I'm afraid of you, Isaiah,
afraid I'll hear the six wings:
Two to cover the face
and two to cover the legs
and two to fly—

And I ask how can I praise
wings that cover feet and face?
And how can I curse
when you have already cursed with your carcasses
of sleazy financiers,
with your ugly and public deaths for those who squeeze
the poor, the widowed, the temporarily weak?

You ask me to compete
head-on with you, and I can't because I cannot hear
in your presence.

You thunder so, in the space inside my left ear,
that I cannot forget you,
even for the length of a line, the weight of a tear.

Wadi

The wind, which is as strong as God, or even stronger,
is what God uses to make the Euphrates
dry as land—

and then the Euphrates becomes seven wadis,
which is interesting, I suppose, if you think wadis
are a good thing, a nice word, and so seven are welcome,

like blessings,
or seven fat years of fat cows,
of good strong wheat,

and your welcome of the word wadi means you've never
walked near one alone, as a girl in Jerusalem, waiting for a rock to hit your head,
the rock of a stranger who makes you forget yourself…
and suddenly an anger you didn't know you had rises inside your heart,

and then you hear a rock, or is it the pounding of fear,
and in the heat you make yourself breathe,
make yourself say, Jerusalem means we will see peace,
and you repeat "Amen, amen, amen" until the sun falls so low
you can no longer see.

Reading Isaiah as my Grandfather's Granddaughter

God will have mercy on Jacob, despite it all—
so there's hope for us humans,
something soothing in the offing.
After all, Isaiah says Babylon's destruction
will mean salvation for Jacob. Tell me, Isaiah,
does redemption always mean destruction
of another? Is that what you mean, just hope
as hard as you can that you are Jacob,
or maybe it just seems that way to me,
the grandchild who should not have been,
whose great-grandparents died so fast,
in the snow, on the border between lands
and destinies, the girl whose grandfather escaped
on the last boat, at the last minute, in the last breaths
before the Mediterranean became red,
before shame forever polluted the blue water.

Ode to Arrogance

With the strength of my arm *I did this*,
with my wisdom with my understanding,
the lie of original poetry as big as the watermelon-big
heart of Sennacherib, big old arrogant king of Assyria,

who roared: the nations I conquered
were lying before me like abandoned eggs—
so many nations, like soil. There was so much
soil, and no one energetic enough to claim it,
so I picked up the earth, I lifted it, *I turned it over.*

Ha! How you laugh at me, Isaiah.
Ha, hoy, ha. In Hebrew and translated English
you guffaw. The ax does not boast; the saw
does not strut. Take the words I gave you,
softly play with the black soil of Iowa,
so fertile it makes farmers weep:

repeat this, you are just the guardian, your name
long and unpronounceable as Assyria,
your stay in this state of wilderness brief,
your arm at the rake and your wrist at the shovel
as fleeting, as hilariously dependent as Sennacherib.

Two Love Songs to Denial

I.

When my wine ends my eye will fall,
meaning my tears will cascade, and I will
look into the desert of my life and wish
for water, little brooks
of hopeful water in the hot dust.

I will wait for men who will shield me from heavy winds,
who will provide shade from the tired earth,
but they will not come, will not run to me fast enough,
will not understand all they need to understand,
and how would they?

How can anyone expect the infinite
from the finite?

And so I will look to the heavens
and beg for a rock, a stone,
the thump and thud of thunder, music,
lightning, presence, a light on a faraway stage.

II.

When I can no longer deny
everything I want to deny, when I have to say—
I chose it, I asked for it, this life I have been given—
this life, the life of a crooner, a bird, a prophet
in the goddamn wilderness,

I picked it for myself,
I chose this fate—

I watched my lips burn and took the loneliness
and the song and the sweat,
I grabbed it, I grabbed it—
I was there, I traded love for music.

Wine

Now that I finally understand what it means
to walk wine-less and with sunburned feet through the pages
of my life, I know with my mouth and my eyes
that I have not died—I have just lived a little.

Esteem

Ephraim's envy shall cease, Isaiah says,
once the wolf dwells with the lamb:
And I take that as saying that jealousy's
here to stay, that's why it's all over
the Ten Commandments, and as I sit
with you at lunch in the little city
I now call home and look at your big
green eyes, the lusciousness of your beard,
the muscles just below your shoulders,
I wonder how you can be envious
of anything, with all that beauty.
I look at you and wonder if love is only
envy accelerated, mutual esteem
amped to the grab of lust, the desire
to possess what beauty another has, to ally
not with the lamb, but the growling wolf.

IV.

All Flesh Is Grass

No One Knows What Happened to the Hittites

Every afternoon he comes to the ruins
to think. Romans, Hittites, Assyrians,
powers mighty and powers long gone,

and still he asks himself questions:
why no great art of his own yet, despite
the decades of sweat and ambition?

"I'm a painter," he tells me before I ask.
"And I'm touring ruins," I say, "to remember
the ancient." Suddenly his wish to unmask

himself seems very old, at least as old
as these amphitheaters of the Romans,
great sandy circles where gladiators

could prove themselves. The painter and I stare
at tall temples to some forgotten god, maybe
the same one who ignored the Hittites' prayers

and let them be eaten alive by the sea peoples,
history's great floating mystery,
who condensed a civilization to rubble.

The painter tells me the Hittites left vases
galore but only sketchy writings, that they
were good people, who were killed hastily.

I think of how long it takes to make something,
and how quickly the Hittites faded into dust.
"Look, see how much is still standing,"

he smiles, motioning to the wide boulevards

for the fat Persian king, the star-filled
mosaics from the shops of Assyria,

and the intricate art that lined the Greeks'
public baths, all of it made by ancients
still whispering *we are here, we were here,*

don't stop asking what happened to us,
we tried to tell you what to expect
but then everything just went bust.

New York

Ask yourselves why you are lying there, far under
the ruins of subway, beneath gray dust of human bone,
in the stench of airplane fuel, rotted teeth, useless paper.

Over many waters, they came to do this to you.
Now what is it that you have done? Isaiah would say
belief has left you, but I am not sure about that, here in the cool

blackness of what once was the building in which I bought
my first stock. Of course stock does not
matter, nor the companies of the day, only the caught

and their howls and moans, the whispered beliefs of the naked
there in the rubble, where the question of prophecy rumbles in bellies.
Earth totters, crumbles: and the dead leave us to wonder, again, in God.

Ode to Humanity as Shimmying Herd

Like sheep that no one gathers,
each of us will waddle back to our people,
to whatever we define as ours,
inching along a path we cannot see
but know by heart. So Isaiah says,
so he wails in his sweet curses,
his melodic pain, that after the rape
of the wives and the ripping
of the children in front of their fathers—
oh how could he imagine the bayonets
of the Reich, the bombs of Jaffa Road?—
after it all, the unspeakable, the abandoned walk back,
because after heaven roars and whinnies,
after earth shimmies and sings, we all still
remain, stuck with our sky and our land
and our desert, with our beating hearts
and the quaking land—and our God,
that errant shepherd, that half-asleep watchman,
accepts all who manage to find him,
and so we come, the left, the abandoned,
shaking our heads: woolly and wild, or utterly shorn.

Night on Wellington Avenue, Chicago

To Germany,
from its German citizens, 1913. Another night
and I am a walker
in the night, a wanderer reading.

The Jewish neighborhood is graced by that odd monument,
and the night is laced with Isaiah, with the juxtaposition
of horrifying prophecy and soft wind.

Is it all exile, all the cities of earth awake
and all the lovers of inexplicable cities walking,
thinking if they just keep moving
it will all be calm,

just keep moving and the body and the mind will exhaust
into sleep?

And I watch as
men hold hands outside a bar,
and women hope for salvation, their whole bodies
one big ear, listening,
asking always that awful phrase
Do you love me? Do you love me?

And as the wind winds
down and the bartender yells last call
I wonder if anyone is really in or if all of us
are always out, out, out, wanderers like
an unwanted prophet, an old man raving.

IV.

All Its Goodness Like Flowers Of The Field

Summer

Summer, finally, and the thunder is thundering
for the fifth day. The weeds are tall as boys,
uncontrollable, thickening and fighting
the idea of order, of summer after spring,
comfort after winter.
My yard in Iowa rules me—
a constant beratement, overgrown,
and I have forgotten most of the words of Isaiah.

Besides—
what good is prophecy in the constant storm,
in this cruel denial of summer?
Humid and wet the earth is,
and only the wolf
and the lamb remain in my mind,
wolf and lamb a refrain like rain,

and maybe that's all there ever was
as I walked through Jerusalem
and New York and Jerusalem again,
my soles exhausted,
ankles and calves burning
in the search for calm—
all my life just lamb and wolf.

Highway

Driving in the fast line, the left lane,
I finally understand
what it is to say "if I forget thee O Jerusalem
let me lose my right hand,"
let me lose all its abilities, all its little strengths,
and I lose hold of the steering wheel
and the tiny car sways like a rudderless ark
in furious waters.
Someone honks
and then drives on, revenge-less,
and I remember that land is not terrible,
no, despite what you warn
us all, Isaiah, nor is the Judaean desert doomed,
but man, that weed, that warrior, that sweetheart,
it is the human who we are fated to fear, trust, beg, thank—
the mortal, driving along the plains of earth.

September Tenth

Just as straw is consumed by the tongue of fire,
so the masked men want me to quake.
So they swagger the day before the disaster,

while I walk higher and higher,
until I can see their eyes, until
the air around me is all blueness

in the mountains of early September.
I stand at the mouth of the hills of Lebanon,
hills festooned with posters of the dead,

young men stolen: now dust
and ire, their faces fluttering in the occasional
wind, and the gun of a masked man

follows me down the main street of Metullah,
the northernmost point of Israel, the last stand.
But the mountains did not shake, or laugh,

and God's anger, that thing Isaiah calls wrath—
that did not come either, and I left swearing to remain
a girl, always, and not a gun-fearing woman—

but the world does not always want a girl. It wants age,
it wants fear, gray hair, sunburn, evidence of strain;
a face that has stared into the open mouth of rage.

Insomnia in Jerusalem

When I hear tank-fire flitting among
the black mountains in flashing arcs of white light,
I sit up in bed, softly bite my tongue

and wonder if I should wake Leah,
the old lady downstairs, the one half-deaf
and so afraid of the sun that she wears

hats all the time, even in the evenings.
In Isaiah, I think I read, the city can explode,
and in its redness it's too late for most women

to be saved. Seven women cling
to one man and beg,
but the only man left is weak,

his skin exhausted, his body cursed
and shaking. When the rounds of fire
squeak and sing and sometimes purr

I want to cling to that familiar
God I grew up with and once believed
would walk with me forever—

but downstairs Leah is asleep,
and counting on me to save her.
For the moment the creaks

of explosion are still distant,
so I get up, find Isaiah, and read him
to the rhythm of the flashing bursts.

Ancient Hebrew

How close the villain is to the harp!
Two vowels separate them, just as two small
letters separate the harp from the generous.

Of course no one learns languages like this,
because it's considered wrong, ridiculous,
but why that is—that's what I want to know.
Yes the villain can be as mesmerizing as the harp,
yes evil can seem generous, in clever disguise. Yes all
of them have their own rhythms, and all are close:
Oh who has not felt the tingling of mischief and crime,
sweet music of generosity and still, the lingering pluck
of am-I-evil, am-I-bad-beneath-it-all?

I am giving and villainous and musical.
In my body I carry clarity and crime and the harp.

Troubadour

Take a violin, oh forgotten slut,
take your songs to the street
and remind your aging lovers
that you were once young—
that you exist, that you can still
be beautiful. Sing as many songs
as you can, sing, oh forgotten one,
until you are hoarse, and in your emptiness
beg to become sweet again.
So Jerusalem washes up
the bones, the heads, the nails,
the blood and hair of the forgotten,
so it forces itself to sing, to praise,
and Manhattan, the first city I knew,
takes the high heels of its women
and tells them to walk, walk faster,
just live, *live*! But still tough men
clamber to make the subways run,
workers work to let the underworld
return. To the naked eye, to the too-young-
to-see, too-young-to-worry, King George
Street and Broadway look smooth,
loud with the hawkings of salesmen.
Shoes and towels, books and fresh fruit—
everywhere in Jerusalem, luscious orange persimmon,
and stocks and bonds in the gleaming city of my girlhood.
Beneath the catcalls of the salesmen,
the workers, the slaves of the underworld,
some of them wearing lace beneath it all,
I hear the feminine wail of violin.

Disco

Tell me—who made the world lie in waste,
who wrecked the villages, one by one,
until only a lone woman was left?

Smoke and fire, music and the tick-tick-tick
of aftermath. In the whitewashed apartment
a mother of two girl dancers has no hair to slick

into buns, no necklaces to fasten at the neck.
The bomb's cheap trick—
to unclasp it all. Who cocked

the trigger, who flicked the switch, who rang
the cell phone that flipped life
into explosion? Once I was a singer who sang

into the black night of the dance floor,
the crystal-ball shine of it.
Now I alone

am left to tell, I alone still have two legs
to walk out into the flower-less
world: I have left the village

of my isolation to tell you
I was a lone woman singing,
dancing in the tick-tick-tick of the wreck,

holding the word Dolphinarium—
saying, daughters, anklets, daughters,
saying this dance of a world
was once my world, this wreck is my world.

Shards

Babylon has fallen, fallen—
and all her idols have collapsed, in delicate detail,
in precise shards. So says the messenger,
so he reports, but I want to know about those shards,
the little pieces, the clay survivors of destruction,
broken and sinning and once-colorful.
Tell me, once split, once shamed,
what did they do next?

Isaiah, you don't say, and the commentators,
my old friends, the squabbling men
of medieval desks, of Aramaic-speaking classrooms,
you don't care either.
You want to know about the messenger,
you're busy imagining Habakkuk
and Koresh or the angel of God,
you want to know whether fallen, said twice,
means Babylon is doomed to fall again—

We all are. All doomed, all poised
to fall.
But I want the details, I want the identities
of the little shards,
their exact addresses and conditions,
I want to visit what
once was a god and became pottery, became shard.

Hallucination

Fatten the heart of the people
until there is total desolation,
Isaiah begs. And I want to know
how desolate is desolate, whether
one son gone is enough, or must it be all
of them, must it be all the cities I have loved
and all the words I have wanted,
all the comfort I have known?
Must I give up my language
and my religion, my God
and my land, the crevices of my body,
as the old man warned me?
"I am old, and I know," he said,
and then held my shaking hand
and said poetry would make
me happy, but only after it had taken
everything else; after it had left
me desolate, my heart thinned
to just words. And so Isaiah let
the angel touch his lips and burn
them, and sometimes I wonder
if I imagined everything, imagined
my entire life, made up the bearded
old man, the magnificent poet
whose words guide me, the man
whose words have made my life
my life, as perhaps Isaiah imagined
he saw God himself on his throne:
the being was holy, holy, holy,
surrounded by fawning angels,
with three pairs of fluttering wings,
and Isaiah knew he would do everything
for that vision, would give up his

life and even his lips, his very mouth.

The Becoming

A hardening hunger, a need.
A billboard along every highway
of the drying soul.

In the imagined life,
the beginning is
hot fire,

but the next steps: becoming—
and then—lasting—are shrouded
like the hills of Jerusalem in the dark.

And so, on nights when
I cannot fathom how to become
all I want to become,

when I can't see
all the lines and lives
I hope to live,

I imagine Isaiah
walking up the parched
hills of Jerusalem in the dark.

He had to have had crises
of the night,
long wakings

of the soul, like all artists.
And I let myself
wonder how he learned
word-fire.

What Remains

Sometimes in the night I still hear it:
a gun, emptying itself into the fields,
a bomb, erupting in the vegetable market

as the first bargain-hunters arrive.
After all these sunburned, tired years
of fighting prophecy, battling Isaiah,

whose songs streamed into my ears at all hours
as I struggled to write my own world,
and swallow the sour seeds of cowardice

and let them be songs. The dead
poets have already left us
all they knew of earth

and flesh, and from inside
the thick white beyond,
they sing with whitened lips

and translucent throats:
Listen closely, mortal one.
To live is a form of music.

Rereading Chapter Eleven

Something is about to dry up the tongue
of the Egyptian sea, just seconds after it looked like
the wolf and the lamb were about to lounge

together. And that's what frightens
me, that God or whoever can just dry it all up,
take it all away, which is what happened

to the brother of the builder of my parents'
house, who had his tongue cut out
of his mouth at Auschwitz, which sent

him into a life without sound, a sentence
of being misunderstood. I think of the tongueless
man every year on Yom Kippur, the holiest

of the holy days, and what makes me tremble
are the words: Lord open my lips
and let my mouth utter your praises. Humble,

it's supposed to sound, and I know I need to ask
for that opening of the lips, and then I remember
the lines before that—man has the inner workings

of the heart, and God owns the tongue.
But I want the tongue, that's all I want,
to have one body part that is mine alone,

to say, God, take it all, control the land,
rule over me all my life, but don't take
that, no, no, don't cut my tongue out, not that.

*

How to Soothe

Speak to Jerusalem tenderly, speak to her heart,
tell her quietly that it's over—

that she's suffered doubly for all her sins.
Tell me, Isaiah, is your repetition confusion,

or just obsession with punishment?
Nachamu, nachamu, comfort oh comfort,

you try later, as if to say, comfort can come
more than once too. And maybe repetition

is just that, comfort, oh and ooh, the hum of it
like earth's sway in the night,

like the space between poetry and prophecy—
ancient, circular, persistent.

NOTES

These poems are all in conversation with two magnificent books: The Book of Isaiah, in the original Hebrew, and H.L. Ginsberg's masterful translation of Isaiah into English, *The Book of Isaiah: A New Translation* (The Jewish Publication Society of America, 1973).

I am also grateful for commentaries from the past two thousand years by writers who have also been fascinated by the Book of Isaiah. These commentaries were written by Avraham Ibn Ezra (1092–1167); the Malbim (1809–1879); Radak, or Rabbi David Kimchi (1160–1235); Ramban, or Nachmanides (1194–1270); Rashi, or Rabbi Shlomo Yitzchaki (1040–1105); and the Mahari Kra (c. 1065–1135) in Hebrew; and Onkelos (c. 35–120) in Aramaic.

Specific references are detailed in these notes:

I. A Voice Rings Out

"The Book of Isaiah": Isaiah 1:2–3.

"Music": Isaiah 16:11.

"Rumor": Isaiah 1:3.

"Chapter 11": Isaiah 11:15.

"Isaiah Starts It Up": Isaiah 1:1 and 1:2. The 11th-century commentator Rashi wonders why only Judah and Jerusalem are mentioned in these verses, when we know that Babylon will come up in Isaiah Chapter 13, and Moab will be discussed in Chapter 15. Rashi suggests that Isaiah 1 is not the true beginning of the book; instead, he thinks the real beginning is Isaiah 6:1. (Other prophetic books like Jeremiah and Ezekiel have first chapters that start with the dedication of a prophet to his task.) Rashi also notes that the Hebrew word "chazon," used in Isaiah 1:1, is the harshest of the ten expressions for prophecy, according to Genesis Rabbah 44:7.

"Smoke": Isaiah 24:1 and Isaiah 36:1.

"The Earth Is Tottering, Tottering": Isaiah 24:19.

II. Proclaim!

"Stupor": Isaiah 12:1.

"The Wind": Isaiah 11:2.

"Storm": Isaiah 40:1–2.

III. Another Asks: What Shall I Proclaim?

"Talking Back to Isaiah": Isaiah 21:4.

"Isaiah Gets Feisty": Isaiah 27:13.

"Why Don't You Write in Hebrew?": Isaiah 6:1–2.

"Wadi": Isaiah 11:15.

"Reading Isaiah as my Grandfather's Granddaughter": Isaiah 14:1.

"Ode to Arrogance": Isaiah 10:13–14.

"Love Song to Denial": Isaiah 32:2 is behind the phrase "tears will cascade."

"Esteem": Isaiah 11:6; Isaiah 11:13.

III. All Flesh Is Grass

"No One Knows What Happened to the Hittites": The Book of Isaiah mentions many once-great powers that no longer exist.

"New York": Isaiah 23:3.

"Ode to Humanity as Shimmying Herd": Isaiah 13:14.

"Night on Wellington Avenue, Chicago": Isaiah 14:7.

IV. All Its Goodness Like Flowers of the Field

"Summer": Isaiah 11:6.

"Highway": Isaiah 21:1–3.

"September Tenth": Isaiah 5:24. On a visit to the Lebanon border in Metullah, Israel, on a very sunny September 10, 2001, posters affixed to the hills featured the faces of three kidnapped Israeli soldiers: two Jewish soldiers and one Druze officer. All were later declared dead.

"Insomnia in Jerusalem": Isaiah 4:1.

"Ancient Hebrew": This poem came from staring at Isaiah 32:5. If the vowels beneath the letters of the word for "villain" in that verse are covered, the word becomes "harp."

"Troubadour": Isaiah 23:16.

"Disco": Isaiah 14:17. The Dolphinarium was a dance club in Tel Aviv, popular with teenagers, that was bombed on June 1, 2001. 21 people were killed, including 16 teenagers; two sisters—Yulia Nelimov, age 16, and Yelena Nelimov, age 18—were among the dead.

"Shards": Isaiah 21:9.

"Hallucination": Isaiah 6:6–7.

"Rereading Chapter 11": Isaiah 11:15.

"How to Soothe": Isaiah 40:1–2.

ACKNOWLEDGMENTS

Grateful acknowledgment is made to the editors of these magazines, where the following poems first appeared, sometimes in earlier versions:

236: "Highway"
Crab Orchard Review: "September Tenth"
Harvard Review: "Isaiah Starts It Up"
The Jerusalem Post: "How to Soothe"
Literary Imagination: "Rumor" and "New York"
Moment: "Music"
Passages North: "Disco"
The Saint Ann's Review: "No One Knows What Happened to the
	Hittites"
Salamander: "Esteem," "Wadi," "Summer" [then titled
	"Comfort"], "Talking Back to Isaiah," "Smoke," "Ancient
	Hebrew,"* "The Wind," "Rereading Chapter Eleven," "Stubble,"
	and "The Book of Isaiah" [then titled "Isaiah From Afar"]

"The Becoming" appeared in *Needing Isaiah's God in Troubled Times: Reflections on Twelve of Isaiah's Words* by Carole Streeter (Xlibris Corp., 2017).

**"Ancient Hebrew"* *was reprinted in* 236; *it was also issued as a broadside by* Salamander.

ABOUT THE AUTHOR

Aviya Kushner grew up in a Hebrew-speaking home in New York. She is the author of *The Grammar of God: A Journey into the Words and Worlds of the Bible* (Spiegel & Grau / Penguin Random House, 2015), which was a National Jewish Book Award Finalist, a Sami Rohr Prize for Jewish Literature Finalist, and one of *Publishers Weekly*'s Top 10 Religion Stories of the year. She is also the author of the poetry chapbook *Eve and All the Wrong Men* (Dancing Girl Press, 2019). Kushner is *The Forward*'s language columnist, and previously wrote a travel column for *The International Jerusalem Post*. She is an associate professor at Columbia College Chicago, a founding faculty member at the Randolph College MFA program, and a member of The Third Coast Translators Collective. Her work has been supported by the Howard Foundation, the Illinois Arts Council, and the Memorial Foundation for Jewish Culture.

ABOUT ORISON BOOKS

Orison Books is a 501(c)3 non-profit literary press focused on the life of the spirit from a broad and inclusive range of perspectives. We seek to publish books of exceptional poetry, fiction, and non-fiction from perspectives spanning the spectrum of spiritual and religious thought, ethnicity, gender identity, and sexual orientation.

As a non-profit literary press, Orison Books depends on the support of donors. To find out more about our mission and our books, or to make a donation, please visit www.orisonbooks.com.

Orison Books wishes to thank Richard Chess, Katie Farris, Ilya Kaminsky, and Sebastian Matthews for their financial support of this book.

For information about supporting upcoming Orison Books titles, please visit www.orisonbooks.com/donate/, or write to Luke Hankins at editor@orisonbooks.com.